# Contents

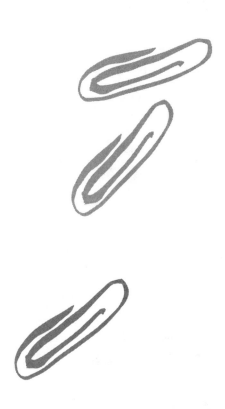

# About This Resource

The ability to convey one's thoughts in writing is an essential skill, necessary for many aspects of our lives. Writing gives us a record of our thoughts, allowing us to stop to reflect, analyze, review, clarify, change, and understand better what we think. Learning about the writing process and how to write effectively is vital for all students.

*Writing and Thinking Skills: Fun with Writing* is a valuable resource for parents and teachers. This book contains a wealth of challenging and stimulating writing activities to challenge middle-grade students. The wide variety of materials will help parents and teachers as they work with students of all ability levels. This excellent resource is published in a format that includes activity pages that are easily reproducible for distribution in classrooms or at home, as well as Student Study Pages with essential information your students can use as a guide in their writing.

## Whom This Resource Is For

The materials in *Writing and Thinking Skills: Fun with Writing* are designed for students in approximately grades 5–8, but can be used with any students who need to improve their writing and thinking skills.

Recent national writing assessments have found that students appear to be gaining basic skills, though most still have difficulty demonstrating that they can apply these skills and use higher levels of thinking that involve analysis. This resource is aimed at the upper-elementary grades because studies suggest that upper-elementary students are less likely to write on their own outside of school. *Writing and Thinking Skills: Fun with Writing* will ensure parents and teachers that their students are gaining and using the writing and thinking skills they need.

## Organization

This resource contains a variety of activities that are fun and interesting for students to practice their writing and thinking skills. Each section includes accompanying teaching material, learning objectives, special extension activities, student study pages, and student activity sheets. The teaching material precedes the practices and contains the following:

Explanation
Learning Objectives
Directions for Student Study Pages and Activities
Extensions

The extension activities are intended to extend learning in each of the skill areas. You may use some or all of these activities as appropriate for your students.

An Assessment Tool Progress Report appears at the end of the book (page 109), as well as a Student Evaluation Progress Report (page 110). You may use either of these reports as is appropriate with your students. They can be copied and used for each student in each skill area. The Student Study Pages and activity pages are also reproducible. The teaching material offers suggestions for record keeping and can be especially helpful for student portfolios.

Reproducible Student Study Pages are provided for students to use throughout the unit. Students can keep these pages available for reference as they work through the unit activities and when they do their own writing.

The student activities for each section are graduated in levels of difficulty. You can choose appropriate activities based on the ability level of each student. Clear and understandable directions are provided for student activities.

## Teaching Suggestions

*Writing and Thinking Skills: Fun with Writing* can be used in a number of ways. The writing activities in this book especially lend themselves to programs geared to help students achieve more rigorous standards. The premise of this writing program is that most students can achieve at higher levels if they are provided the proper teaching and help.

This special writing book features many creative writing activities that require high-level thinking. Though students will be practicing the writing and thinking skills essential to writing effectively, they will also have fun by using their imaginations and creativity in these enjoyable, interesting activities.

I encourage you to continuously assess your students' writing behavior. You can gain information about your students' writing by using observation and student portfolios as well as, when appropriate, other informal and formal diagnostic measures. You then can use this data to either reinforce, supplement, enrich, or develop skill and strategy areas.

You are the decision maker. You must determine, based on the developmental levels of your students, which concepts and the amount of instruction you need to provide.

Section 1

# PUNCTUATION AND SENTENCES

## Explanation

This section is a review of punctuation and sentence writing skills that reinforce the materials presented in this special writing and thinking book. You may want your students to do the review activities provided here before proceeding onto the challenging writing activities throughout.

## Learning Objectives

Students should be able to:

- recognize that the placement of punctuation marks in a sentence can change the meaning of the sentence
- correct sentences with misplaced modifiers
- unscramble sentences so that they make sense
- make at least ten sentences from the given list of words
- combine sentences to make new sentences
- generate sentences in which the first letter of each word is the next letter of the alphabet
- write a one-sentence tongue twister and then write their own tongue twisters

## Directions for Student Study Pages and Activities

Use the activity pages (pages 14–32) to help your students acquire, reinforce, and review punctuation and sentences. Make copies of the reproducible Student Study Pages on pages 11–13 for each student. This section can be used as reference while they do the punctuation and sentence activities, as well as when they do their own writing.

# PUNCTUATION AND SENTENCES

You can pick and choose the activities based on the needs and developmental levels of your students. Answers for the activity pages are reproducible, so you may choose to give your students the activity pages as well as the answer pages to let them progress on their own. The answers are on pages 115–117.

## Extensions

- Write a specific amount of each of several punctuation marks on the board. For example, write "4 periods, 1 question mark, 7 commas, 1 semicolon, and 1 exclamation point" on the board. For this example, ask each student to write a silly, six-sentence paragraph about any topic he or she chooses, using only the punctuation marks listed on the board. Students can then read their silly paragraphs aloud.

- Have sentence races! Write words and punctuation marks on pieces of posterboard and cut them out. Or you may want to purchase word magnets. Divide the group into two teams. Team members try to come up with a coherent sentence by using the word and punctuation cards. Write each team's sentences as they create them, so that the words and punctuation cards or magnets can be used again. The team that has the greatest number of sentences in a specific time period is the winner. To make the game more difficult, announce a specific sentence type before each round, such as a simple sentence, compound sentence, and so on.

- Create paragraph puzzles for your students. Type between 50 to 100 random words on a sheet of paper. Include common words, such as "and," "a," "I," and "the," often throughout the scrambled paragraph. Print a copy of the page for each student and challenge them to use as many of the words as they can to create a coherent paragraph. Children can cross off each word as they use it. They may use each word only once.

- Make cryptograms for the students to decipher. A *cryptogram* is a sentence or paragraph written in code. Write messages, ideas, or thoughts for the day in a cryptogram and challenge students to "break the code." For example:

    It is an equal failing to trust everybody as to trust nobody.

becomes

    Pa pl or qsnob yopbprc af aedla qmqehifth ol af aedla rfifth.

Name _____

# Student Review for Punctuation and Sentences

## Punctuation

**Directions:** Place the proper punctuation within each sentence.

1. Though I didnt care I still wanted to go

2. Hey watch where youre going

3. Jose said Im not doing that mom

4. Is that yours Janes or mine

5. Im not going to tell you said Jack even if you beg

6. Who are you talking to asked Sarah as she turned to look behind her

## Sentences

### Combining Sentences
**Directions:** Write one sentence that combines the two sentences in each of the following pairs. Use a comma with the words *or, but,* or *and* in the sentences you write.

1. I would like to go to college.
   My grades are not as good as I would like.


2. I can get better grades.
   I know I can work harder at my studies.


### Shortening Sentences
**Directions:** Shorten the following sentences, using commas.

1. Ty likes to cook. Sasha likes to cook. Jenny likes to cook.

2. Salvatore and Jake and Tiffany are in a book club together.

**Independent and Dependent Word Groups**
**Directions:** Underline the dependent word group in each of the following sentences.

1. Val loves the rain because it helps her plants grow.

2. Anahid's Dad drove Caitlin to her house when she needed a ride.

**Combining Independent and Dependent Word Groups**
**Directions:** Combine the two sentences in each of the following pairs. Use one of the linking words from the list. Add necessary commas.

Linking Words:     although     because     even though     if     when

1. We didn't drink the tea.
   We were thirsty.

2. They can get better seats.
   They get to the concert early.

**Adjectives and Adverbs**
**Directions:** Fill in each blank with the correct adjective or adverb.

1. Gregory is _____ , but Katie is the _____ .
   (faster, funniest, funny)

2. The _____ play was performed _____ by the cast.
   (wonderfully, exciting, quickly)

# Student Study Pages

## Punctuation and Sentences

## Punctuation

When you speak, your voice, your facial expressions, and your body movements help give meaning to what you are saying. Punctuation marks are the signals that help give meaning to what you write. Here are the punctuation marks that you will be working with in the activities that follow:

- **.**      **period**
- **?**      **question mark**
- **!**      **exclamation point**
- **,**      **comma**
- **;**      **semicolon**
- **" "**      **quotation marks**

### Commas
A comma signals a pause. This pause is not as strong as the stop signaled by a period (.).

### Semicolons
When linking words such as *also, therefore, so, moreover, however, then,* and *nevertheless* join two simple sentences to form a compound sentence, a semicolon is usually used before the linking word.

### Quotation marks
Quotation marks (" ") are always used when you write a direct quotation or titles of poems, songs, stories, articles, and chapters. Quotation marks are NOT used when you write an indirect quotation.

## Sentences

### Simple Sentences
A simple sentence is made up of a word or group of words that names something (subject) and says something about the thing named (predicate). It expresses a complete meaning or thought. A simple sentence, which expresses one complete thought, can be written with a compound subject (two or more) and a single verb, with a single subject and a compound verb, or with a compound subject and a compound verb.

## Student Study Pages *continued*

### Compound Sentences

A compound sentence is made up of two or more simple sentences. Two simple sentences may be joined by linking words called *conjunctions* to form compound sentences. Conjunctions that connect groups of words that have the same importance are called *coordinating conjunctions.*

### Complex Sentences

A complex sentence is made up of one simple sentence and one or more groups of words that cannot stand alone as sentences. In order to understand a complex sentence, you must be familiar with the terms *independent clause* and *dependent clause.* A *clause* is a group of words that contains both a subject and a predicate.

### Independent Clause

A clause that makes an independent statement is an *independent clause.* An independent clause can stand alone as a simple sentence because it expresses a complete thought. For example, "Kelsey is pretty, and Peter is handsome." (*Kelsey is pretty* is an independent clause, and *Peter is handsome* is also an independent clause.)

### Dependent Clause

A clause that is not by itself complete in meaning is called a *dependent clause.* A dependent clause cannot stand alone as a sentence because it does not express a complete thought. For example, "Although he is very tall, he didn't make the basketball team." (*Although he is very tall* is a dependent clause, and *he didn't make the basketball team* is an independent clause.) A complex sentence contains one independent clause and one or more dependent clauses.

### Subordinating Conjunction

Linking words, called *subordinating* (dependent) *conjunctions,* connect dependent clauses with their independent clauses to form complex sentences. The most often-used subordinating conjunctions are the following words: *although, as, because, before, if, since, that, unless, until, after, as if, as though, even though, even if, as soon as,* and *so that.* Pronouns such as *who, which, that,* and *what* can also function as subordinating conjunctions to connect a dependent clause to an independent clause.

### Compound-Complex Sentences

A compound-complex sentence is made up of two or more independent clauses and one or more dependent clauses. The only difference between a compound-complex sentence and a complex sentence is that a compound-complex sentence has two or more independent clauses.

## Student Study Pages *continued*

### Sentence Expansion with Modifiers

Sentences can be expanded or enlarged by adding words that modify (describe or limit) nouns and verbs. The descriptive words that modify nouns or pronouns are called *adjectives*. The descriptive words that modify verbs are called *adverbs*.

### Combining Sentences

Good writers often balance simple sentences with longer and more involved ones. More important ideas are presented in principal or independent clauses, and less important ideas are presented in dependent clauses. The following are examples of the various ways that sentences can be combined or joined together.

1. Jack is athletic. Jack is intelligent.

   Jack is athletic and intelligent (simple sentence).

2. Tony likes rock music. Tony likes classical music.

   a. Tony likes rock and classical music (simple sentence).

   b. Although Tony likes rock music, he also likes classical music (complex sentence).

3. The finals were very difficult. We passed all of them.

   a. Although the finals were very difficult, we passed all of them (complex sentence).

   b. The finals were very difficult, but we passed all of them (compound sentence).

   c. Although we passed all of them, the finals were very difficult (complex sentence).

   d. The finals were very difficult; nevertheless, we passed all of them (compound sentence).

4. The finals were very difficult. We passed all of them. Some of our friends flunked them.

   We passed all of the finals, which were very difficult, but some of our friends flunked them (compound-complex sentence).

Name _____

# Punctuation Riddles 1

**Directions:** Here are five sets of sentences. See how well you can answer each question for each set of sentences. Then write the correct letter on each blank. (Hint: Check the punctuation.)

1.  a. My sister Molly is pretty.
    b. My sister, Molly, is pretty.

    In which is there only one sister? _____

2.  a. Did you see that he crossed the line?
    b. Did you see that! He crossed the line!

    Which is an accusation? __B__

3.  a. Ms. Smith, the principal wants to see me.
    b. Ms. Smith, the principal, wants to see me.

    In which is Ms. Smith the principal? _____

4.  a. Mr. Brown says, "My sister is a lawyer."
    b. "Mr. Brown," says my sister, "is a lawyer."

    In which is Mr. Brown a lawyer? __B__

5.  a. Did you ever see a knee jerk?
    b. Did you ever see a knee, jerk?

    In which is someone addressed in a belittling way? __A__

Name _____

# Punctuation Riddles 2

**Directions:** Here are five sets of sentences. See how well you can answer each question for each set of sentences. Then write the correct letter on each blank. (Hint: Check the punctuation.)

1.   a. Are you saving, Jane?
     b. Are you saving Jane?

     In which could Jane be thrifty? _____

2.   a. Mr. Smith says, "John is wealthy."
     b. "Mr. Smith," says John, "is wealthy."

     In which is Mr. Smith wealthy? _____

3.   a. I saw a man-eating fish.
     b. I saw a man eating fish.

     Which would you avoid meeting? _____

4.   a. Children, listen to me.
     b. Children listen to me.

     In which are the children listening? _____

5.   a. Look at the lady clown.
     b. Look at the lady, clown.

     Which lady would you find at the circus? _____

Name _____

# Punctuation Fun 1

**Directions:** Here are five sentences. A change in punctuation will change the meaning of each sentence. A clue to the new sentence meaning is given in the parentheses. Change the punctuation. (Incomplete sentences are allowed.)

1.  Mother, the plumber fixed the leak. (Make Mother the plumber.) ——————

    _Mother the plumber, fixed the leak._

    _____

2.  Private! No entry at any time. (Change to an open invitation.) ——————

    _____

    _____

3.  The teacher called the students' names as they entered the bus. (Make the

    teacher behave in a very unprofessional manner.) ——————

    _____

    _____

4.  Stop people on the highway. (Show a warning.) ——————

    _____

    _____

5.  Pardon impossible; to be sent back to jail. (Grant the pardon.) ——————

    _____

    _____

*16*

Name_____

# Punctuation Fun 2

**Directions:** Here are five sentences. A change in punctuation will change the meaning of the sentence. A clue to the new sentence meaning is given in the parentheses. Change the punctuation.

1. Jack, the judge said that we could go. (Make Jack the judge.) _____

    _____

    _____

2. I'm not stupid. (Make someone feel dumb.) _____

    _____

    _____

3. Mr. Stein, my teacher, gives too many exams. (Make Mr. Stein the person to

    whom you are complaining.) _____

    _____

    _____

4. My sister, Cara, will be visiting Florida. (Show that you have many sisters.)

    _____

    _____

5. After the ball game we can eat, Susan. (Show that we are cannibals.) _____

    _____

    _____

Name_____

# Ridiculous Sentences 1

**Directions:** Here are five ridiculous sentences. Rewrite the sentences and change their punctuation so that they make better sense. The statement in the parentheses should help you.

1. The man ran after the dog smoking a pipe. (Take the pipe away from the dog.)

   _____

   _____

2. The child is bouncing the ball chewing gum. (Stop the ball from chewing.)

   _____

   _____

3. The girl looked for her sweater crying uncontrollably. (Stop the sweater from crying.)

   _____

   _____

4. The man answered the phone wrapped in a towel. (Unwrap the phone.)

   _____

   _____

5. Jack bought a new car smiling broadly. (Remove the smile from the car.)

   _____

   _____

*18*

Name _____

# Ridiculous Sentences 2

**Directions:** Here are five ridiculous sentences. Rewrite the sentences and change their punctuation so that they make better sense. The statement in parentheses should help you.

1.  The little girl walked into the store eating candy. (Take the candy away from the store.)

    _____

    _____

2.  The speaker gave his lecture twitching nervously. (Stop the lecture from twitching.)

    _____

    _____

3.  The father purchased a great quantity of groceries carrying the baby. (Stop the groceries from carrying the baby.)

    _____

    _____

4.  John watched the movie eating popcorn. (Take the popcorn away from the movie.)

    _____

    _____

Name _____

# Ridiculous Sentences 3

**Directions:** Here are five ridiculous sentences. Rewrite the sentences and change their punctuation so that they make better sense. The statement in parentheses should help you.

1. My hand felt warm in my pocket shivering from the cold. (Stop the pocket from shivering.)

   _____

   _____

2. Roberto planted the tree with itchy eyes. (Cure the tree.)

   _____

   _____

3. Mr. Kinney boarded the bus talking continuously. (Quiet down the bus.)

   _____

   _____

4. The baby banged the carriage crying hysterically. (Stop the carriage from crying.)

   _____

   _____

5. The student wrote on the chalkboard chewing gum. (Take the gum away from the chalkboard.)

   _____

   _____

Name_____

# Ridiculous Sentences 4

**Directions:** Here are five ridiculous sentences. Rewrite the sentences and change their punctuation so that they make better sense.

1. The child was put in the ambulance burning with fever.

   _____

   _____

2. Sherry walked down the street eating an ice cream cone.

   _____

   _____

3. Mr. Dupont mowed his lawn wearing a bathing suit.

   _____

   _____

4. The girl picked up the phone laughing aloud.

   _____

   _____

5. Mrs. McGregor climbed the stairs breathing heavily.

   _____

   _____

Name_____

# Ridiculous Sentences 5

**Directions:** Here are five ridiculous sentences. Rewrite the sentences and change their punctuation so that they make better sense.

1.  Emma jumped over the rope holding her books.

    _____

    _____

2.  Mr. Hoskins took a drink from the water fountain perspiring from the heat.

    _____

    _____

3.  The little girl drew with chalk on the sidewalk singing a song.

    _____

    _____

4.  The mail carrier put the mail in the box coughing excessively.

    _____

    _____

5.  Sarah worked on the computer chewing gum.

    _____

    _____

22

Name _____

# Scrambled Sentences 1

**Directions:** Here are nine scrambled sentences. Unscramble each sentence so that it makes sense. Hint: Each sentence is a well-known proverb.

1. May April flowers showers bring. _____

   _____

2. Ship rats sinking a desert. _____

   _____

3. That gold not is all glitters. _____

   _____

4. Leap look you before. _____

   _____

5. Bite seldom dogs barking. _____

   _____

6. Company people known are keep by they the. _____._____

   _____

7. Meat poison another person's person's is one. _____

   _____

8. Feet grass your under don't the let grow. _____

   _____

9. Success succeeds nothing like. _____

   _____

Name_____

# Scrambled Sentences 2

**Directions:** Here are nine scrambled sentences. Unscramble each sentence so that it makes sense. Hint: Each sentence is a well-known proverb.

1. Deep beauty is skin only. _____

   _____

2. Saves nine a in stitch time. _____

   _____

3. Early worm bird the catches the. _____

   _____

4. Many broth cooks too the spoil. _____

   _____

5. Ape king's ape an clothing in still is an. _____

   _____

6. Trees big from acorns grow little. _____

   _____

7. Book cover by judge don't a its. _____

   _____

8. Wind an that ill blows no one good any it's. _____

   _____

9. Basket all eggs don't your put one in. _____

   _____

Name_____

# Brainstorming Sentences 1

**Directions:** See how many sentences you can make by using the words listed below. Each word may be used only the number of times it appears in the word list. You should be able to make at least six sentences.

**Word list:** a, a, a, acrobats, am, and, and, animals, at, away, be, came, children, circus, clowns, cold, day, do, does, dog, elephant, enjoy, few, funny, hungry, I, I, make, my, my, night, on, or, our, rainy, ran, scared, star, story, the, the, the, tired, to, to, town, tricks, wanted, was, watching, we, were, you.

_____

_____

_____

_____

_____

_____

_____

_____

_____

_____

_____

_____

_____

_____

_____

Name _____

# Brainstorming Sentences 2

**Directions:** See how many sentences you can make by using the words listed below. Each word may be used only the number of times it appears in the word list. You should be able to make at least ten sentences.

**Word list:** a, a, able, am, although, and, and, and, are, are, as, away, bag, blue, boy, can, car, care, carry, cat, child, clothes, cold, day, dog, dressed, far, food, funny, girl, green, happy, help, hungry, hurt, I, I, it, light, long, make, many, me, my, of, old, on, out, pretty, rain, ran, ran, red, run, since, sun, slept, talked, talking, tall, the, the, the, time, to, to, to, together, train, very, walk, walked, warm, was, we, wear, which, white, who, with, you, young.

• A hungry cat dressed warm

• Altough it was cold the train car

_____

_____

_____

_____

_____

_____

_____

_____

_____

_____

_____

_____

Name_____

# Generating Sentences Game 1

**Directions:** Below are two groups of sentences. Make as many sentences as possible with information from each group. Each sentence must be correct and make sense. You may use only information that appears in the sentences in each group. The person with the greatest number of correct sentences is the winner.

**Example:** Group 1—The old man walks slowly.

Group 1:  The man is old. The man walks slowly. The man uses a cane. It is raining. The man is tired. The man is wet.

Because the man is old he slowly walks
with a nice cane. Sadly it is raining
so the man is wet, and therefore tired.

Group 2:  The girl is tall and thin. She has dark hair. The girl is involved in an argument. The girl starts to get angry. Someone tries to help the girl. The girl walks away.

Tall, thin, and dark hair is how to
describe the girl. Involved in an
argument, the girl gets angry. Amazingly,
someon tries to help the girl but still
she walks away.

Name_____

# Generating Sentences Game 2

**Directions:** Below are two groups of sentences. Make as many sentences as possible with information from each group. Each sentence must be correct and make sense. You may use only information that appears in the sentences in each group. The person with the greatest number of correct sentences is the winner.

**Example:** Group 1—The poor children have no parents.

Group 1:  The children are poor. They are tired. The children have no parents. The children are hungry. The children would like to be adopted. The children are not happy. The children run away.

_____

_____

_____

_____

_____

_____

Group 2:  The flowers are pretty. The flowers smell sweet. It is a lovely summer day. Children are playing in the park. People admire the flowers. A child picks a flower.

_____

_____

_____

_____

_____

Name_____

# Generating Sentences Game 3

**Directions:** Below are two groups of sentences. Make as many sentences as possible with information from each group. Each sentence must be correct and make sense. You may use only information that appears in the sentences in each group. The person with the greatest number of correct sentences is the winner.

**Example:** Group 1—The smiling man calls out to his friend.

Group 1:  The man calls out to his friend. The man is smiling. The man is holding a fishing pole. The man is sitting in his truck. It is Saturday. It is a sunny day. The friend gets into the truck. The man wants to go fishing.

_____

_____

_____

_____

_____

_____

Group 2:  The animals are wild. The animals live in the forest. The animals hunt for food in packs. The animals kill farmers' chickens. The farmers want to trap the animals. The farmers hunt the animals.

_____

_____

_____

_____

_____

Name_____

# Generating Nonsense Alphabet Sentences Game

**Directions:** Generate as many sentences as you can in which the first letter of each word in the sentence begins with the next letter of the alphabet. You can begin with any letter of the alphabet, and each sentence must be at least three words long. Each word in the sentence counts for one point, and each sentence counts for three points. The person with the greatest number of points is the winner. (Be sure to set a time limit.)

**Example:** A big cat doesn't eat frankfurters.

_____

_____

_____

_____

_____

_____

_____

_____

_____

_____

_____

_____

Name _____

# Writing Tongue Twisters to Tangle Tongues 1

**Directions:** Tongue twisters are hard to say because almost every word begins with the same sound. Write one sentence that will twist your friends' tongues.

**Examples:**  She sells seashells at the seashore.

Donny Deardrain dropped darling Diana's dimpled doll down the drain.

Bella banced of the building on bee boulder street.

Name _____

# Writing Tongue Twisters to Tangle Tongues 2

**Directions:** Tongue twisters are hard to say because almost every word starts with the same sound. Write some tongue twisters that will tangle your friends' tongues.

**Examples:**     A tutor who tooted a flute

Tried to tutor two tooters to toot.

Said the two to the tutor,

"Is it harder to toot,

Or to tutor two tooters to toot?"

Peter Piper picked a peck of pickled peppers,

A peck of pickled peppers Peter Piper picked.

If Peter Piper picked a peck of pickled peppers,

Where is the peck of pickled peppers Peter Piper picked?

_____

_____

_____

_____

_____

_____

_____

_____

_____

# RHYME AND POETRY

### Explanation

Poetry expresses the imagination with a rhythmic arrangement of words. Here are some examples of limericks, newspaper poetry, concrete poems, cinquains, and haiku.

### Limerick

Limericks are supposed to be funny, silly, and ridiculous. They consist of a five-line pattern. The first, second, and fifth lines rhyme with one another and have three beats. The third and fourth lines also rhyme with one another and have two beats. For example:

> There was a young fellow named Fisher,
> Who was fishing for fish in a fissure.
> > Then a cod with a grin
> > Pulled the fisherman in . . .
> Now they're fishing the fissure for Fisher.

### Concrete Poetry

A concrete poem needs an object to be the central focus of the poem, such as a ball, truck, flower, or even fingers. The object becomes part of the poem, and the words of the poem are arranged around or within the object. The arrangement of the words and the object chosen should express the feeling of the poem.

### Newspaper Poetry

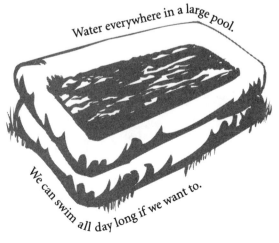

Water everywhere in a large pool.

We can swim all day long if we want to.

© Good Apple GA13081

Newspaper poets, like concrete poets, are concerned with the arrangement of words on a page. However, in newspaper poetry more importance is given to the arrangement and appearance of the words rather than with a specific object. (See page 48 for examples.)

## Cinquain

Cinquains are based on a five-line pattern. Although there are a number of different patterns, the most often used is 1-2-3-4-1. The first line has one word; the second, two; the third, three; the fourth, four; and the fifth, one. Each line usually has a purpose:

**Line 1** states the theme of the cinquain poem.
**Line 2** describes the theme of the poem.
**Line 3** provides an action for the theme.
**Line 4** gives a feeling of the theme.
**Line 5** states another word for the theme.

For example:

> Rain
> soft drizzle
> falls on plants
> quiet splashes of water
> Growth.

## Haiku

Haiku is one of the oldest forms of Japanese poetry. Unlike cinquains, which are patterns of words, haiku is based on syllables. Haiku consists of three lines composed of seventeen syllables—five in the first line, seven in the second line, and five again in the third line. The most important factor in haiku poetry is the feeling that is being portrayed in the poem. Themes in haiku are usually about beauty and nature. For example:

> Light dance on water
> hopping from ripple to wave
> Flickering light fades.

## Learning Objectives

Students should be able to:

- write a nonsense sentence that rhymes with a given sentence and then write their own nonsense poem
- write the last two lines of a given limerick and then write their own
- write a newspaper poem with words from newspapers and magazines

- write a newspaper poem with words from newspapers and magazines
- write a concrete poem
- write a cinquain poem
- write a haiku poem

## Directions for Student Study Pages and Activities

Use the activity pages (pages 38–50) to help your students acquire, reinforce, and review rhyme and poetry. Make copies of the reproducible Student Study Pages on pages 36 and 37 for each student. This section can be used as reference while they do the poetry and rhyme activities, as well as when they do their own writing.

You can pick and choose the activities based on the needs and developmental levels of your students. Answers for the activity pages are reproducible, so you may choose to give your students the activity pages as well as the answer pages to let them progress on their own. The answers are on page 117.

## Extensions

- Write one word on the board, such as *horse, breathless, mountain,* or *laugh.* Ask students to use the word as the basis for a poem, limerick, concrete poem, cinquain, or haiku.

- Create a group book of poems. Students can create any form of poetry to include in the book. Find out how you can self-publish the book. You can also contact copy centers in your area to see what it would take to "publish" a copy of the book of poetry for each of your students. Books can be placed in the school library after they are finished.

- Have a poetry reading. Serve refreshments and invite other students and adults to attend. Challenge your students to read their poetry aloud for their guests.

Name _____

# Student Study Pages

## Rhyme and Poetry

### Limerick

Limericks consist of a five-line pattern. The first, second, and fifth lines rhyme with one another and have three beats. The third and fourth lines also rhyme with one another and have two beats. For example:

> There was a young fellow named Fisher,
> Who was fishing for fish in a fissure.
> > Then a cod with a grin
> > Pulled the fisherman in . . .
> Now they're fishing the fissure for Fisher.

### Concrete Poetry

A concrete poem needs an object to be the central focus of the poem. The words can be arranged around or within the object and the words and object should express the feeling of the poem. For example:

Water everywhere in a large pool.

We can swim all day long if we want to.

# Student Study Pages *continued*

## Newspaper Poetry

Newspaper poets, like concrete poets, are concerned with the arrangement of words on a page. However, in newspaper poetry more importance is given to the arrangement and appearance of the words rather than with a specific object. (See page 48 for examples.)

## Cinquain

Cinquains are based on a five-line pattern. Although there are a number of different patterns, the most often used is 1-2-3-4-1. The first line has one word; the second, two; the third, three; the fourth, four; and the fifth, one. Each line usually has a purpose: Line 1 states the theme of the cinquain poem. Line 2 describes the theme of the poem. Line 3 provides an action for the theme. Line 4 gives a feeling of the theme. Line 5 states another word for the theme.
For example:

Rain

soft drizzle

falls on plants

quiet splashes of water

Growth.

## Haiku

Haiku is one of the oldest forms of Japanese poetry. Unlike cinquains, which are patterns of words, haiku is based on syllables. Haiku consists of three lines composed of seventeen syllables—five in the first line, seven in the second line, and five again in the third line. The most important factor in haiku poetry is the feeling that is being portrayed in the poem. Themes in haiku are usually about beauty and nature. For example:

> Light dance on water
> hopping from ripple to wave
> Flickering light fades.

Name_____

# Writing Nonsense Rhymes 1

**Directions:** Below are five nonsense sentences. For each nonsense sentence, write another nonsense sentence that rhymes. The first has been done for you.

1. The bunny hopped into bed.
   It bumped its head.

2. The rat said, "Arf, arf" to the cat.

   _____

   _____

3. The elephant jumped on my lap.

   _____

   _____

4. The ant chased the silly, big hen.

   _____

   _____

5. The beard itched the cat's chin.

   _____

   _____

Name_____

# Writing Nonsense Rhymes 2

**Directions:** Below are five nonsense sentences. For each nonsense sentence, write another nonsense sentence that rhymes. The first has been done for you.

1. The rooster said, "Peep, peep."
   "I need my sleep."

2. The turtle left its shell.

   _____

   _____

3. The giraffe stood on its head.

   _____

   _____

4. The silly wren flew into the pen.

   _____

   _____

5. The dog's tail was a mile long.

   _____

   _____

Name_____

# Writing Nonsense Poems 1

**Directions:** Below is a nonsense poem. See if you can complete the last two lines. Then write your own nonsense poem.

**As I Watch a Flutterfly**

As I watch a flutterfly,
Fluttering on a flowerby
Oh dear, I mean a butterfly
Buttering on a blowerfly.

_____

_____

_____

_____

_____

_____

_____

_____

*40*

Name_____

# Writing Nonsense Poems 2

**Directions:** Below is a nonsense poem. See if you can complete the last two lines.
Then write your own nonsense poem.

**The Anteater and the Parking Meter**

Once there was an anteater
Who tried to use a tark peter.
Oh no, I mean an anterpark
Who tried to use an eatertark.
How'er it goes, he got his nose
Entangled in the park-ter-mose.
The more he tried to jerk it loose,
The louder clinked the meter phoose.

_____

_____

_____

_____

_____

_____

_____

_____

*41*

Name_____

# Writing Limericks 1

**Directions:** Limericks consist of a five-line pattern. The first, second, and fifth lines of a limerick rhyme with one another, and the third and fourth lines rhyme with one another. The first, second, and fifth lines have three beats, whereas the third and fourth lines have two beats. Limericks are supposed to be funny, silly, and ridiculous.

**Example:**     There was a Young Lady of Norway,
                    Who casually sat in a doorway;
                         When the door squeezed her flat,
                         She exclaimed, "What of that?"
                    This courageous Young Lady of Norway.

*Edward Lear*

Now try to write two different last lines for the above limerick.

1. _____

_____

2. _____

_____

*42*

Name_____

# Writing Limericks 2

**Directions:** Below is an incomplete limerick. Supply the last two lines. Remember that the third and fourth lines rhyme with one another and that the first, second, and fifth lines rhyme with one another. Remember also that limericks are supposed to be funny, silly, and ridiculous.

> There was an Old Man in a tree,
> Who was horribly bored by a bee;
> When they said, "Does it buzz?"

1. _____

_____

2. _____

_____

Name_____

# Writing Limericks 3

**Directions:** Below is an incomplete limerick. Supply the last two lines. Remember that the third and fourth lines rhyme with one another and that the first, second, and fifth lines rhyme with one another. Remember also that limericks are supposed to be funny, silly, and ridiculous.

There was an old man of Tobago,

Lived long on rice gruel and sago;

But at last, to his bliss,

1. _____

_____

2. _____

_____

44

Name_____

# Writing Limericks 4

**Directions:** Below are two incomplete limericks. Supply the last two lines. Remember that the third and fourth lines rhyme with one another and that the first, second, and fifth lines rhyme with one another. Remember also that limericks are supposed to be funny, silly, and ridiculous.

> There was an Old Man with a beard,
> Who said, "It is just as I feared!
> Two Owls and a Hen,

1. _____

_____

2. _____

_____

> There was an old person of Ware,
> Who rode on the back of a bear;
> When they asked, "Does it trot?"

1. _____

_____

2. _____

_____

Name _____

# Writing Limericks 5

**Directions:** Write your own limerick. Remember that the third and fourth lines rhyme with one another and that the first, second, and fifth lines rhyme with one another. Remember also that limericks are supposed to be funny, silly, and ridiculous.

_____

_____

_____

_____

_____

_____

_____

46

Name_____

# Fun with Concrete Poetry

**Directions:** Choose an object or objects to be the central focus of your poem, such as a ball, truck, flower, or even your own fingers. The object becomes part of your poem, and you can arrange the words of your poem around or within your object. The arrangement of your words and the object you use should express your feeling.

**Example:**

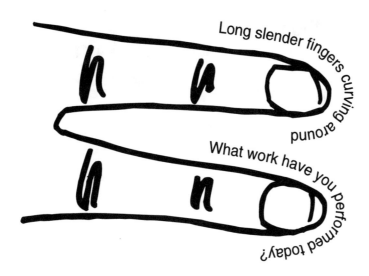

Long slender fingers curving around

What work have you performed today?

Now write one of your own.

Name_____

# Newspaper Poetry Writing Fun

**Directions:** Choose words from newspapers and magazines that express certain feelings or thoughts. These words can be of various sizes, shapes, and colors. Arrange the words in a pattern that best expresses your thought or feeling.

**Examples:**

**D**emons of the Night

These visions, which

haunt

are

sinister,

terrifying

## Beyond

fantasy

The

**Strangers in**

darkness

,

**a Strange Land**

far away

from

laughter

## DARK .

Now write one of your own.

*48*

Name_____

# Cinquain Fun

**Directions:** Cinquains are based on a five-line pattern. The most often used is 1-2-3-4-1. The first line consists of one word; the second, two; the third, three; the fourth, four; and the fifth, one.

**First line:** states the theme.
**Second line:** describes the theme.
**Third line:** provides an action for the theme.
**Fourth line:** gives a feeling of the theme.
**Fifth line:** states another word for the theme.

**Example:**

Fog,

white blanket

covering the universe

how still and quiet

Peace.

Now write some cinquains of your own.

Name_____

# Haiku Fun

**Directions:** Haiku is one of the oldest forms of Japanese poetry. It consists of three lines composed of seventeen syllables—five in the first and third lines and seven in the second. The most important factor in haiku poetry is the feeling that is supposed to be portrayed in the poem. The themes are usually concerned with beauty and nature.

**Example:**

The Morning Mist

The morning mist crept (5 syllables)
over my lawn as I slept (7 syllables)
at the crack of dawn. (5 syllables)

Now write some haiku of your own.

_____

_____

_____

_____

_____

# CHALLENGES IN WRITING

## Explanation

Creative writing and basic skills are not mutually exclusive. The more knowledge writers have of the mechanics and practical aspects of writing, the more creative they usually can be. This section concentrates on a combination of practical and creative writing.

## Definitions

**Figures of speech** are special ways of using words. They are important because they give color, decoration, and life to language. Some figures of speech, called *idioms,* are quite common. We use them without realizing it, because they have become part of everyday language. The following are examples of idioms: *the body of a letter, the foot of the mountain, the hands of a clock, the heart of the matter,* and *take it on the chin.*

Understanding figures of speech is necessary to the appreciation of most poetry, as well as other literature. The figures of speech most commonly used in writing are *simile, metaphor, personification, hyperbole,* and *oxymoron.*

A **simile** is a comparison of two unlike objects. It uses the words *like* or *as.* The following are some examples of similes:

> The clouds are like marshmallows in the sky.
> Her hair is as black as night.
> Jake ran toward Paulo like an angry bull.

A **metaphor** compares two unlike objects *without* using the words *like* or *as.* For example:

> The clouds are marshmallows in the sky.
> Eyes are windows into the soul.
> The snow is a blanket of white.

**Personification** is the giving of human characteristics and capabilities to non-human things, such as inanimate objects, abstract qualities, or animals. The following are some examples of personification:

> The blue water called out to the swimmers.
> The dog looked at her with his big brown eyes and pleaded for a bone.
> After a long, tiring day, the overstuffed couch embraced me in its warm comfort.

**Hyperbole** is excessive exaggeration. Writers use hyperbole for effect. For example:

> I cried a river of tears.
> It took him forever to finish the project.
> This package weighs a ton!

An **oxymoron** is a figure of speech in which contradictory terms are combined for effect in writing, as in the following:

> There was a deafening silence.
> The party was a sad celebration.
> Jake was a cold person with a warm heart.

This section also has activities dealing with descriptive words such as adjectives and adverbs. **Adjectives** are words that describe or limit nouns and pronouns—for example, *pretty* child. **Adverbs** are used to describe or limit verbs or adjectives—for example, run *fast*.

In addition, this section includes some creative, challenging activities dealing with **compound words,** which consist of separate words that combine to form a new word. Compound words may appear as one-word compounds (grandfather), two-word compounds (river bank), multiword compounds (maid of honor), or hyphenated compounds (right-of-way).

A number of activities are also devoted to homonyms (homophones). **Homonyms** (or **homophones**) are words that sound the same, but have a different spelling and mean different things, such as the words *red* and *read, weather* and *whether,* and *pale* and *pail* in these sentences:

> Rhonda *read* a book with a *red* cover.
> I don't know *whether* the *weather* will change or not.
> Jill was very *pale* as she carried the *pail* up the hill.

### Learning Objectives

Students should be able to:

- solve riddles involving figures of speech
- choose a word or phrase from a list that most vividly completes a simile and then create their own similes

- choose a word or phrase from a list that most vividly completes a metaphor
- choose a word or phrase from a word list that most vividly portrays an expression of personification
- write expressions of personification for given words or phrases and put each in a sentence
- write a descriptive sentence using hyperbole
- complete each sentence with an oxymoron
- write five oxymorons and put each in a sentence
- use given clues to figure out a compound word and then use the word in a sentence
- write three adjectives for each letter of their name
- generate ten different words for each underlined word
- change the given words into another part of speech as specified
- change incorrectly spelled homonyms (homophones) so that the sentence makes sense

## Directions for Student Study Pages and Activities

Use the activity pages (pages 56–74) to help your students acquire, reinforce, and review writing challenges. Make copies of the reproducible Student Study Page on page 55 for each student. This section can be used as reference while they do the challenges in writing activities, as well as when they do their own writing.

You can pick and choose the activities based on the needs and developmental levels of your students. Answers for the activity pages are reproducible, so you may choose to give your students the activity pages as well as the answer pages to let them progress on their own. The answers are on pages 117–119.

## Extensions

- Challenge students to find figures of speech in newspapers, magazines, and books they are currently reading. Ask them to keep a list of the figures of speech as they read. Post the figures of speech on a bulletin board or ask students to share them with the rest of the group. See who can come up with the most figures of speech in a given time period. Remind students that they are looking for similes, metaphors, personification, hyperbole, and oxymorons.

- Invite students to write similes about each other. Stress that they are to only write positive similes about each person in the group. For example:

    Sarah is as smart as a fox.
    Grant's able to run like a sailboat in a strong wind.
    When Sabrina throws a ball, it sails through the air like an eagle.

# CHALLENGES IN WRITING

■ Write a number of sentences containing one homonym. Make a copy of all the sentences onto one sheet of paper for each student. Ask students to come up with the homonym that matches the one in the sentence and create another related sentence with the new homonym. For example:

The sun is in my eyes.
I can see your house from here.
My aunts are coming to visit.

Tell my son to bring me my sunglasses.
It must be nice to live by the sea.
I hope I can get rid of the ants before they get here.

Name _____

# Student Study Page

## Challenges in Writing

### Some definitions of terms:

**Figures of speech**   Give color, decoration, and life to language. We often use figures of speech called *idioms* without realizing it because they have become part of everyday language. Example: The foot of the mountain. The figures of speech most commonly used in writing are *simile, metaphor, personification, hyperbole,* and *oxymoron.*

**Simile**   A comparison of two unlike objects that uses the words *like* or *as.* Example: Her hair is as black as night.

**Metaphor**   A comparison of two unlike objects *without* the use of the words *like* or *as.* Example: Eyes are windows into the soul.

**Personification**   The giving of human characteristics and capabilities to nonhuman things, such as inanimate objects, abstract qualities, or animals. Example: The shimmering blue water called out to the swimmers.

**Hyperbole**   An excessive exaggeration. Example: I cried a river of tears.

**Oxymoron**   A figure of speech in which contradictory terms  are combined for effect in writing. Example: There was a deafening silence.

**Adjectives**   Describe or limit nouns and pronouns. Example: *pretty* child.

**Adverbs**   Describe or limit verbs and adjectives. Example: run *fast.*

**Compound words**   Separate words that combine to form a new word. Compound words may appear as one-word compounds (grandfather), two-word compounds (river bank), multiword compounds (maid of honor), or hyphenated compounds (right-of-way).

**Homonyms (or homophones)**   Words that have the same sound, but have different spellings and mean different things, such as the words *red* and *read, weather* and *whether,* and *pale* and *pail.* "I don't know whether the weather will change or not."

Name _____

# Figure of Speech Riddles 1

**Directions:** Below are six figure of speech riddles. Answer each question and then state the idiom to which the riddle refers. The first has been done for you.

1. Which part of the body is in front of the class?

   Head _____

   head of the class _____

2. What plant does each family grow to tell about its ancestry?

   _____

   _____

3. What part of a bottle can cause a traffic jam?

   _____

   _____

4. Which stalk of grain causes people to give up?

   _____

   _____

5. Which part of the body does a journey possess?

   _____

   _____

6. What do you climb to reach fame and fortune?

   _____

Name_____

# Figure of Speech Riddles 2

**Directions:** Below are six figure of speech riddles. Answer each question or state the idiom to which the riddle refers.

1.  Which parts of the body does a clock have?

    _____

    _____

2.  When is an apple not a fruit but part of your body?

    _____

    _____

3.  What flower bed makes life soft and easy?

    _____

    _____

4.  When do you wear a millstone as a necklace?

    _____

    _____

5.  In what kind of a chase is a goose never found?

    _____

    _____

6.  What part of the body, when it's cold, ignores you?

    _____

    _____

Name _____

# Simile Fun 1

**Directions:** Below are ten sentences with a missing word or phrase. Choose a word or phrase from the word list that most accurately and vividly completes a simile. Remember, a simile is a comparison between two unlike objects that uses the words *like* or *as*.

**Word or phrase list:** (a) a glowing orange ball; (b) a winding snake; (c) marshmallows; (d) a razor's edge; (e) a light in the night; (f) a seal; (g) a waterfall; (h) a swift bird; (i) a tall bride; (j) a telegraph

1. The clouds are like _____ floating in the sky.

2. Her tears flowed like _____ .

3. The woodpecker's pecking sounded like _____ tapping out a message.

4. From the airplane, the dirt road looked like _____ .

5. Her sharp disposition is as cutting as _____ .

6. The doe is like _____ in flight.

7. The answer illuminated the subject like _____ .

8. He looked like _____ with his drooping whiskers and bald head.

9. The sun rose as _____ in the east.

10. The white birch looked like _____ .

*58*

Name_____

# Simile Fun 2

**Directions:** Complete each of the following similes. In Part 1, add only one word or phrase. In Part 2, add two words or two phrases. Remember, a simile is a comparison of two unlike objects that uses the words *like* or *as*.

Part 1  **Example:** Her skin is as dry as leather.

1. A book is like a(n) _____.

2. Her golden hair is as bright as _____.

3. The fog is like a(n) _____.

4. My hands are as rough as _____.

5. Her words were as sharp as _____.

6. His bald head looks like a(n) _____.

7. The eagle swooped upon its prey like _____.

8. My emotions are as drained as _____.

9. Her dress is as crumpled as _____.

10. He is as wet as _____.

Part 2  **Example:** His whiskers are as bristly as a porcupine.

1. _____ is as cold as _____.

2. _____ is as bitter as _____.

3. _____ is as dark as _____.

4. _____ are as exhausted as _____.

5. _____ is as bright as _____.

Name _____

# Metaphor Fun 1

**Directions:** Below are ten sentences with a missing word or phrase. Choose a word or phrase from the word list that most accurately and vividly completes a metaphor. Remember, a metaphor compares two unlike objects without using *like* or *as*.

**Example:** The book is a ship that takes us to faraway lands.

**Word or phrase list:** (a) a ghost; (b) an erupting volcano; (c) a mashed potato; (d) a bird with clipped wings; (e) caged birds; (f) spitballs of fire; (g) a miner excavating a mine; (h) diamonds; (i) bloodhound; (j) porcupine.

1. To me the dentist is _____.

2. A grounded pilot is _____.

3. Her angry words were _____.

4. After the crowded train ride, I was _____.

5. He is _____ of his former self.

6. The hostages were _____.

7. When she's angry, she's _____.

8. My father's _____ whiskers tickle my skin when he kisses me.

9. Her eyes are _____ that sparkle in the night.

10. His _____ nose led us immediately to the spot.

Name_____

# Metaphor Fun 2

**Directions:** Below are ten sentences with a missing word or phrase. Choose a word or phrase from the word list that most accurately and vividly completes a metaphor. Remember, a metaphor compares two unlike objects without using *like* or *as*.

**Example:** My face became a beet when John caught me glancing at him.

**Word or phrase list:** (a) daggers; (b) a shield of armor; (c) a wet sponge; (d) putty; (e) a veil; (f) a powder keg; (g) a rocket; (h) leather; (i) a peacock; (j) a blanket.

1. Everyone becomes _____ in the coach's hands.

2. _____ was firmer than her sincerity.

3. The sun had made _____ out of his skin.

4. The fog spread _____ of white mist on the ground.

5. Our mother's heart becomes _____ when we start making certain requests.

6. Her remarks were _____ piercing my heart.

7. He is _____ ready to explode at any moment.

8. John is _____ who tries to attract all the girls.

9. The idea was _____ that struck me when I least expected it.

10. _____ fell across her eyes when she heard the news.

Name _____

# Personification Fun 1

**Directions:** Below are ten sentences with a missing word or phrase. Choose a word or phrase from the word list that most accurately and vividly portrays an expression of personification. Remember, personification is the giving of human characteristics and capabilities to nonhuman things.

**Example:** The dry earth begged for water.

**Word or phrase list:** (a) stared; (b) groaned; (c) danced brilliantly; (d) greedily drank; (e) turned its face; (f) crept slowly; (g) beat its fists; (h) put on its cloak of darkness; (i) shed its tears; (j) refused.

1. The flower _____ toward the sun.

2. The couch _____ as the three women sank deeply into it.

3. The wind _____ against my window.

4. My car _____ to budge.

5. The fire _____ in the night.

6. The dry earth _____ the water.

7. The sun _____ at the ship for hours on end.

8. The fog _____ along the ground.

9. As the candle _____, it grew smaller and smaller.

10. It would soon be time for the day to _____ .

Name _____

# Personification Fun 2

**Directions:** Write an expression of personification for each of the following words and then put each in a sentence. Remember, personification is the giving of human characteristics and capabilities to nonhuman things.

**Example:** Clouds—The angry clouds opened their mouths, and a torrent of rain came out.

1. Sun _____

   _____

   _____

2. Cars _____

   _____

   _____

3. Flowers _____

   _____

   _____

4. Ships _____

   _____

   _____

5. Stuffed chair _____

   _____

   _____

Name_____

# Hyperbole Fun

**Directions:** Write a descriptive sentence, using hyperbole (excessive exaggeration) for each of the following topics.

**Examples:**

Getting dressed—It takes me ages to get dressed in the morning.

Weight—This thing weighs a ton!

1. Eating _____

   _____

   _____

2. Sleeping _____

   _____

   _____

3. Fear _____

   _____

   _____

4. Travel _____

   _____

   _____

5. Being happy _____

   _____

   _____

Name _____

# Oxymoron Fun 1

**Directions:** Below are five sentences missing words. Fill in each sentence with an appropriate oxymoron. Remember, oxymorons are word opposites. They are used to attract our attention and for effect.

**Example:** The silence was so loud that everyone knew something was wrong.

1. Dracula awakens _____

   _____ .

2. After many sleepless nights, Ryan looked like _____

   _____ .

3. She is _____ ,
   even though she is so wealthy.

4. Some persons feel that love is _____

   _____ .

5. The losses on both sides were so great that _____

   was _____ .

Name_____

# Oxymoron Fun 2

**Directions:** Write five oxymorons and put each into a sentence. Remember, oxymorons are word opposites.

**Examples:**

Bittersweet—I have bittersweet memories of my childhood days, which were filled with love and poverty.

Friendly enemies—The candidates of the opposing parties are many times friendly enemies.

_____

_____

_____

_____

_____

_____

_____

_____

_____

Name_____

# Compound Words Fun 1

**Directions:** Use the given clues to figure out the compound word. Then write a sentence using the word.

1. A part of the body plus drinking containers (you wear these).

   _____

   _____

2. A part of the body plus something you can stand in (a newspaper uses this).

   _____

   _____

3. A part of the body plus a kind of fancy cloth (a piece of jewelry).

   _____

   _____

4. A part of the body plus a tool pointed at one end (restaurants have this).

   _____

   _____

5. A part of the body plus something round that bounces (a game).

   _____

   _____

Name_____

# Compound Words Fun 2

**Directions:** Use the given clues to figure out the compound word. Then write a sentence using the word.

1. A part of the body plus the opposite of *in* (beggars want this).

_____

_____

2. A part of the body plus something you can eat (a tree).

_____

_____

3. A part of the body and what fire does (you don't want this).

_____

_____

4. A part of the body plus three feet (land behind a house).

_____

_____

5. A part of the body plus *to fasten* (a decorative piece of clothing).

_____

_____

Name_____

# Descriptive Word Fun

**Directions:** For each letter of your name, write three adjectives.

**Example:**

| | | | |
|---|---|---|---|
| J | jolly | joyous | jumpy |
| A | able | amorous | arty |
| C | careful | clever | calm |
| K | kind | kingly | keen |

———————— ———————— ———————— ————————
———————— ———————— ———————— ————————
———————— ———————— ———————— ————————
———————— ———————— ———————— ————————
———————— ———————— ———————— ————————
———————— ———————— ———————— ————————
———————— ———————— ———————— ————————
———————— ———————— ———————— ————————
———————— ———————— ———————— ————————
———————— ———————— ———————— ————————
———————— ———————— ———————— ————————
———————— ———————— ———————— ————————
———————— ———————— ———————— ————————

Name_____

# Descriptive Word Sentence Fun

**Directions:** Generate at least five different words for each of the italicized words in the sentence "The *man moved* out of the *place.*" Then the words should be placed in a sentence.

**Example:** Words — *thief, ran, bank*

The *thief ran* out of the *bank.*

1. *man*

_____

_____

_____

_____

_____

2. *moved*

_____

_____

_____

_____

_____

3. *place*

_____

_____

_____

_____

_____

Name

# Word Endings Fun

**Directions:** Below are a list of word endings. Use the word endings to change the words or phrases that follow the list into other parts of speech. The word in parentheses will tell what part of speech the word should be changed to. Then write a sentence using the new word.

**Example:** Dirt (adjective) + -*y* = dirty:  The little boy always seemed to get dirty.

**Word endings**: *-ic, -y, -ous, -tion, -al, -ed, -ize, -ment, -dom, -ly, -ice, -ish, -fy, -ace, -ity, -ty, -ness, -ism, -ence, -ance, -or, -er, -ar, -ship, -en, -ure*

1. To act (noun) —————————————————————

   —————————————————————————————

2. To play (noun) ————————————————————

   —————————————————————————————

3. Polite (adverb) —————————————————————

   —————————————————————————————

4. Trick (adjective) ————————————————————

   —————————————————————————————

5. Nice (adverb) —————————————————————

   —————————————————————————————

6. Charming (adverb) ———————————————————

   —————————————————————————————

7. Prince (adjective) ————————————————————

   —————————————————————————————

8. Free (noun) ——————————————————————

   —————————————————————————————

9. Fair (adverb) —————————————————————

   —————————————————————————————

Name_____

# Homonym (Homophone) Sentence Fun 1

**Directions:** Below are five sentences. Change whatever words you have to so that each sentence makes sense.

1. My I hurt on the plain.

   _____

   _____

2. Eye eight a hole stake.

   _____

   _____

3. Did you sea the bare run into the woulds?

   _____

   _____

4. Eye no that the weigh two root ate is knot this weigh.

   _____

   _____

5. Eye rote two my ant to tell her sun two right two me.

   _____

   _____

Name _____

# Homonym (Homophone) Sentence Fun 2

**Directions:** Below are five sentences. Change whatever words you have to so that each sentence makes sense.

1. Eye no that the sealing has a leek.

   _____

   _____

2. My friend is a vein, lien person who likes two lye in the son at the beech.

   _____

   _____

3. Eye eight currents, pares, and carats.

   _____

   _____

4. The principle mist hour class.

   _____

   _____

5. Know won aloud the course person two enter hour meeting.

   _____

   _____

Name_____

# Homonym (Homophone)
# Sentence Fun 3

**Directions:** Below are five sentences. Change whatever words you have to so that each sentence makes sense.

1. Eye am the soul person inn the coral seen that does knot sing.

   _____

   _____

2. Eye no too people who lye allot.

   _____

   _____

3. Know won will bye the choral canvass tent because it has an odd sent.

   _____

   _____

4. The principle inn hour mane building does knot no hour kneads.

   _____

   _____

5. Ate workers on lone from won other school were scent two fix hour building.

   _____

   _____

74

Section 4

# JOKES, TALL TALES, AND STORIES

## Explanation

Students can use the writing skills they have learned about writing paragraphs and compositions in the creative writing activities provided in this section.

A **story** is usually defined as a series of related events or happenings. It is an account of something that may or may not have happened. Some stories are true and others are not. However, most stories are created to entertain readers or listeners. Stories should have a beginning, middle, and end. The **beginning** usually describes the characters and background of the story. The **middle** adds events and characters that move the story along. The **end** gives the story a conclusion, bringing the characters and events together in a logical and cohesive manner.

A **joke** is supposed to make people laugh. It is often like a miniature story. Writing jokes can be great fun for your students. A joke is usually funny because it says the opposite of what the reader or listener expects.

A **tall tale** is an exaggerated, incredible, and improbable story. Tall tales can be about anything at all, and students can let their imaginations roam as they write their tall tales.

**Dialogue** is conversation in a play, movie, or story. Students can create dialogue for their characters in their stories by imagining what each character they have created might say.

## Learning Objectives

Students should be able to:
- write the final line for incomplete jokes
- write a tall tale
- choose or make up a fascinating question and then write a tall tale to answer the question

- choose an "If I . . ." phrase and then write a story about it
- use imagination to combine any animal with any object to create a rare animal and then write something funny about it
- invent an animal and then use imagination to write about it, explaining everything about it
- imagine that they are television producers and come up with a new kind of show
- write a review of a television show
- write a new ending for an episode of the television show of their choice
- choose characters from a television show for a possible spin-off and write about what kind of show the spin-off will be
- choose a ridiculous topic and write a funny story about it
- choose an idea that appeals to them and write a short story about it
- choose a nonsense title that appeals to them and write a story about it
- write an ending for a given story
- choose a fairy tale and write another ending for it
- complete a story with dialogue

## Directions for Student Study Pages and Activities

Use the activity pages (pages 79–98) to help your students acquire, reinforce, and review writing jokes, tall tales, and stories. Make copies of the reproducible Student Study Page on page 78 for each student. This section can be used as reference while they do the story activities, as well as when they do their own writing.

You can pick and choose the activities based on the needs and developmental levels of your students. Answers for the activity pages are reproducible, so you may choose to give your students the activity pages as well as the answer page to let them progress on their own. The answers are on pages 119 and 120.

## Extensions

- Challenge students to write short skits. Explain that they will only be able to use dialogue to tell their stories in the skits. Invite groups to present their skits in front of the rest of the students.

- Invite students to write memoirs. Explain to students that a memoir is writing about something that actually happened to them. Students can choose an event or series of connected events from their lives they would like to share. Then ask those students that would like to share their memoirs to read them to the rest of the group.

■ Write group or partner stories. Divide the group of students into partners or teams of three or more. One student can begin a story with a sentence or two, or even a short paragraph. He or she then passes the story on to his or her partner or another person in the group.  That person continues the story. The students pass the story between them or among their group to complete the story. After approximately ten to fifteen minutes, ask the students to share their group or partner stories.

Name _____

# Student Study Page

## Jokes, Tall Tales, and Stories

A **story** should have a beginning, middle, and end. The **beginning** usually describes the characters and background of the story. The **middle** adds events and characters that move the story along. The **end** gives the story a conclusion, bringing the characters and events together in a logical and cohesive manner.

A **joke** is supposed to make people laugh. It is often like a miniature story. A joke is usually funny because it says the opposite of what the reader or listener expects.

A **tall tale** is an exaggerated, incredible, and improbable story. Tall tales can be about anything at all. They allow the writer to use his or her imagination.

**Dialogue** is conversation in a play, movie, or story. Writers can create dialogue for characters by imagining what each character might say.

Name_____

# Writing Jokes 1

**Directions:** Writing jokes can be fun. You can also use your jokes to get a laugh out of your friends. It's not hard to write jokes if you understand what makes a joke funny. A joke is usually funny because it says the opposite of what you would expect. This can happen if the most important part of the joke is not written but left to your imagination. For example, this joke is funny because what you expect to follow doesn't.

*Customer:*    Waiter, my soup has a fly in it.

*Waiter:*    That's okay. We didn't charge you for it.

Here are some other jokes that are funny because of surprise endings or double meanings.

*Passenger:*    I can't bear to watch you driving so fast around corners. It makes me nervous.

*Driver:*    Keep your eyes closed, madame. I'd be scared, too, if I looked.

A man telephoned a doctor, asking him to rush over at once. His son had swallowed a fountain pen.

"I'll come at once," said the doctor, "but what are you doing in the meantime?" "I'm all right," the man replied. "I'm using a pencil."

Now complete these jokes to make them funny:

1. "Well, well, well, you must have grown a foot since I saw you last," said the uncle to his nephew.

_____

_____

2. The customer said, "I hope you can count on that."

_____

_____

Name_____

# Writing Jokes 2

**Directions:** Write final lines for the following incomplete jokes. Remember that the most important part of a joke is not what is written but what is left to the reader's imagination.

1. Customer: You have a very clean place here, don't you?

    Waiter: Yes, we scrub everything with soap every day.

    Customer: _____

    _____

2. Student: I don't think I deserve a D on this paper.

    Teacher: _____

    _____

*80*

Name_____

# Writing Jokes 3

**Directions:** Write final lines for the following incomplete jokes. Remember that the most important part of a joke is not what is written but what is left to the reader's imagination.

1. Mother: Did you change the water in the goldfish bowl?

   Child: _____

   _____


2. Sarita: Did you know that it took a number of silkworms to make this beautiful silk dress?

   Jennifer: _____

   _____

Name _____

# Writing Jokes 4

**Directions:** Write final lines for the following incomplete jokes. Remember that the most important part of a joke is not what is written but what is left to the reader's imagination.

1. Jim: Next week we're going to visit the place where they mint money.

   Ahmad: _____

   _____


2. Child: Is it true that the law of conservation of energy keeps energy on this planet constant?

   Teacher: Yes.

   Child: _____

   _____

Name_____

# Fun with Tall Tales

**Directions:** A tall tale is a highly exaggerated, incredible, and improbable story. Tall tales are fun to write because you can really let your imagination roam. You can make up a tall tale about an object, an event, a person, an animal, and so on.

## Example:

Before the dinosaurs came from Venus, a giant came from Mars. He was fifteen miles tall and not very smart. When he lay down, he made the English Channel. He took his bath in the Indian Ocean, and he went swimming in the Atlantic Ocean. After his swim, when he put his hand on land, he made the Great Lakes. When he sat down to eat lunch, he made the Grand Canyon. Then he amused himself by making sand castles. These sand castles became the Great Smoky Mountains. After a while, he went back for another swim. This time, he made all of the valleys, and he broke a dam, which let the ice from the Arctic into the United States. This made all of our glaciers.

Now you write a tall tale!

_____

_____

_____

_____

_____

_____

_____

_____

_____

_____

_____

_____

_____

_____

_____

Name_____

# Fascinating Questions 1

**Directions:** Below are a number of fascinating questions. Choose one and then create a tall tale to answer the question.

Why do monkeys eat bananas?

Why do zebras have stripes?

Why are snakes limbless?

Why is grass green?

Why does the ocean have salt water?

Why do lions roar?

Why does a camel have a hump on its back?

Why do birds fly?

Why do people talk?

Why are there clouds in the sky?

Why do ducks quack?

Why do bees sting?

Why do snakes hiss?

Why are ants social insects?

Why do mountains have ice caps?

Name_____

# Fascinating Questions 2

**Directions:** Make up your own "fascinating question" and then write a tall tale to answer it.

**Examples:**

Why do leopards have spots?     Why does the moon come out at night?

Why is the earth round?     Why do dogs bark?

_____

_____

_____

_____

_____

_____

_____

_____

_____

_____

_____

_____

_____

_____

_____

_____

_____

_____

_____

_____

Name_____

# If I...

**Directions:** Below are a number of "If I..." phrases. Choose one that appeals to you and write a story about it.

If I could foretell the future...

If I were the strongest person in the world...

If I could remember everything that I read...

If I had strange powers...

If I were marooned on a strange island...

If I were president...

If I lived on the moon...

If I were the only human being on earth...

If I had magic power...

If I could be...

If I had...

If I could fly...

If I were twenty feet tall...

If I were no bigger than a speck...

If I were the smartest person in the world...

_____

_____

_____

_____

_____

_____

_____

_____

_____

_____

_____

_____

_____

_____

Name_____

# Scrambled Animal Fun 1

**Directions:** In the book *The Ice Cream Cone Coot* by Arnold Lobel, there are many strange and rare birds. The author has combined bird parts with everyday objects to make some unusual birds. For example, he has combined a pencil and a parrot to make a Pencilkeet Parrot, a dollar bill and a dodo to make a Dollarbill Dodo, and a water glass and a goose to make a Water Glass Goose. You can use your imagination to combine any animal with any object to make your own special rare animal. Describe your animal and tell something funny about it.

_____

_____

_____

_____

_____

_____

_____

_____

_____

_____

_____

_____

_____

_____

_____

_____

_____

_____

_____

Name _____

# Scrambled Animal Fun 2

**Directions:** Have you ever wondered what a fish would look like with a chicken's head or what a snake would look like with ducks' legs? You don't have to anymore. You can use your imagination to invent your very own animal. Describe your animal and tell why you made it the way you did. Write about your animal's special habits, where it lives, and its characteristic sound or way of communicating. Then draw a picture of it.

_____

_____

_____

_____

_____

_____

_____

_____

_____

_____

_____

_____

_____

_____

_____

_____

Name _____

# Television-Writing Fun 1

**Directions:** Imagine that you are a television producer. The ratings on a number of your shows have been going down. You need to come up with a new kind of show that will appeal to a lot of people. What kind of show would you come up with? Describe it.

_____

_____

_____

_____

_____

_____

_____

_____

_____

_____

_____

_____

_____

_____

_____

_____

_____

_____

Name _____

# Television-Writing Fun 2

**Directions:** Imagine that you are a television reviewer. Choose a new situation comedy show and write a review of it. Here are some guidelines you can use in writing your review:

1. Did the show maintain your interest? Explain.

2. How did the actors perform their roles?

3. Was the plot original? Explain.

4. Is the show similar to others? Explain.

5. Was there anything special about this show? Explain.

6. For what audience is this show?

7. Would you choose to watch this show over others? Explain.

8. How does this show compare to others of its type?

_____
_____
_____
_____
_____
_____
_____
_____
_____
_____
_____
_____
_____
_____

Name_____

# Television-Writing Fun 3

**Directions:** Imagine that you are a television scriptwriter. Choose a show that you have seen on television and write a different ending for it.

_____

_____

_____

_____

_____

_____

_____

_____

_____

_____

_____

_____

_____

_____

_____

_____

_____

_____

_____

_____

_____

Name _____

# Television-Writing Fun 4

**Directions:** Imagine that you are a television producer with a lot of hit shows. You are thinking of making a spin-off of one of your shows. Choose a television show that you think has possibilities for a spin-off. Choose the characters that you would use in your spin-off and describe what kind of show it would be.

_____

_____

_____

_____

_____

_____

_____

_____

_____

_____

_____

_____

_____

_____

_____

_____

_____

_____

Name_____

# Ridiculous Topics

**Directions:** Below are some ridiculous topics. Choose one that appeals to you and write a funny story about it.

The butter that refused to melt.

The cow that was allergic to milk.

The mirror that disliked reflections.

The oven that couldn't stand the heat.

The cloud that disliked moisture.

The rooster that liked to sleep late.

The scarecrow who liked crows.

The light who hated to be turned out.

The kangaroo without a pouch.

The refrigerator that was allergic to food.

The umbrella that was afraid of the rain.

The telephone that refused to ring.

The lion who couldn't roar.

The flower who was allergic to noses.

The button that disliked thread.

The cat that barked.

The dog that meowed.

The lion that said, "Peep, peep."

The monkey that was afraid of heights.

The salad that hated dressing.

_____

_____

_____

_____

_____

_____

_____

_____

_____

_____

_____

_____

Name _____

# Short Story Ideas

**Directions:** Below are a number of ideas for a short story. Choose one that appeals to you and write a short story about it. Or, you can come up with your own idea!

I was changed into a fish and lived in a fishbowl.

The television set that talks back.

A person who lives in a walnut shell.

A magic fan.

A computer that can talk.

A person with extraordinary power.

The radio that remembers everything said in its presence.

The people who live in the sea.

_____

_____

_____

_____

_____

_____

_____

_____

_____

_____

_____

_____

_____

_____

_____

_____

_____

94

Name_____

# Nonsense Titles

**Directions:** Below are a number of nonsense titles. Choose one that appeals to you and write a story about it. Or you can come up with your own idea.

The Dingle That Ploobed          A Visit to Velanious

A Peropious Gragle               My Flaggled Nooble

Two Seripitious Flangles         The Werancious Who Zooled the Hansiplous

_____

_____

_____

_____

_____

_____

_____

_____

_____

_____

_____

_____

_____

_____

_____

_____

Name _____

# Ending a Story 1

Here is a synopsis of Frank R. Stockton's famous story "The Lady or the Tiger?" Read it carefully and then write your own ending for the story.

Many years ago, a barbaric king punished crime or meted out rewards by decrees of impartial chance. When a subject was accused of a crime of sufficient importance to warrant the notice of the king, notice was given and a day appointed on which the fate of the accused would be determined. All persons would gather on that day and assemble in the galleries, while the accused would be below in the king's amphitheater. In front of the accused were two doors exactly alike and side by side. The person on trial had to choose one. Behind one door was a ferocious, hungry tiger who would spring on its victim and immediately devour him. Behind the other door was a fair and beautiful maiden, who would then become the accused person's bride.

The king's daughter, unknown to the king, was in love with one of his courtiers. When the king discovered this romance, he threw the handsome young man into prison, because no subject was allowed to love the princess. The appointed day for the youth's trial came. The princess sat next to her father. She had learned the secret of the doors and knew that her father had chosen one of the fairest and loveliest of all maidens to wed the accused youth if he chose her door. Her lover knew she would learn the secret of the doors, and from the arena he looked at her. The princess, unnoticed by anyone but the youth, raised her right hand. The youth, without hesitation, opened the right-hand door.

Now the question is this: Did the tiger come out of that door, or did the lady?

_____

_____

_____

_____

_____

_____

_____

_____

96

Name_____

# Ending a Story 2

**Directions:** Have you ever wanted to change the ending of a story? Now is your chance. Choose one of your favorite fairy tales or stories and change its ending.

_____

_____

_____

_____

_____

_____

_____

_____

_____

_____

_____

_____

_____

_____

_____

_____

_____

_____

_____

_____

Name_____

# Completing a Story with Dialogue

Michael had studied very hard for the history exam. He wanted to do well because he had done poorly on all of the other tests. He needed a good grade in this course so that he could try out for the soccer team. His parents said that if he failed any course, he would not be allowed to try out. Well, he had studied for this one, and he felt confident that he could do well on it.

Just as Michael was going to class, one of his friends, who was also interested in trying out for the team, stopped him.

"Hey, wait up," said Ben.

"Hurry," Michael said, "I don't want to be late for class. We're having an exam, you know."

"Of course, I know. That's why I want to talk to you," said Ben. "I need your help. I didn't have time to study, and I really need to do well on this exam. Since you said that you were going to study hard for this exam, I figured that you would let me copy from you. Write big so that I can see," said Ben.

What do you think Michael said? Complete this story with dialogue.

_____

_____

_____

_____

_____

_____

_____

_____

_____

_____

_____

_____

# WRITING LETTERS

## Explanation

Most people enjoy receiving letters. Often, in order to receive a letter, one must write a letter. One may write a friendly letter to a friend or relative. There is also a special form for business letters.

## Letter to a Friend

The **heading** of a friendly letter may give the writer's address as well as the date. Or, the letter writer may choose to only write the date. The **greeting** of the letter states to whom the letter is being written, such as "Dear Marisa." The **body** of the letter presents the letter writer's message, and the **closing** of a letter is a way to say goodbye. The **signature** tells the person receiving the letter who wrote it. In a friendly letter, usually only the first name is given.

Monday, June 3

Dear Marisa,

    It was so good to see you at the park the other day. It's been a long time. How have you been? Have you seen our friend Jerome lately? What's he up to?

    I'm having a few people over for dinner next week. Would you like to come? Please let me know. I would love to see you again.

Fondly,<br>Sharene

## Business Letter

A business letter is more formal, contains more information, and includes an inside address. Business letters are often written flush left—heading, inside address, greeting, body of letter, closing, and signature all at the left-hand margin.

    The **heading** includes the writer's address and the date. The **inside address** includes the title of the person to whom the letter is being sent and his or her address. The **greeting** is more formal and includes the name and title of the person receiving the letter. If the name or title of the person is not known, he or she may be addressed in the greeting as *Dear Sir or Madam* or *To Whom It May Concern*. The greeting is followed by a colon (:). The **body** of a business letter contains the message of the letter, written more formally than in a letter to a friend. The **closing** of a business letter is more formal as well. The most common closings are *Sincerely yours, Sincerely, Yours truly,* or *Cordially*. The **signature** of a business letter is formal, usually including the writer's complete name, handwritten beneath the closing and then printed or typed out below that.

4540 Sacramento Blvd.
Napa, CA 94558
June 3, 2001

Sirs Import and Export, Inc.
798 Hogan Street
Newark, NJ 12345

To Whom It May Concern:

I have not received the three cartons of heirloom seeds I ordered from your company three weeks ago. I would appreciate it if this problem could be taken care of as soon as possible.

Sincerely yours,

*Carol Stradley*

Carol Stradley

## Learning Objectives

Students should be able to:

- write a letter complaining about a commercial from the viewpoint of the product being advertised
- write a letter complaining to a student from the viewpoint of an object ordinarily found in a classroom
- write a letter to a company about a malfunctioning part from the viewpoint of the appliance
- write a letter to a friend, explaining why he or she resembles a storybook character
- write an actual letter to a friend, relative, newspaper, or other person or company in hopes of receiving a reply

## Directions for Student Study Pages and Activities

Use the activity pages (pages 104–108) to help your students acquire, reinforce, and review writing letters. Make copies of the reproducible Student Study Pages on pages 102 and 103 for each student. This section can be used as reference while they do the letter-writing activities, as well as when they do their own writing.

You can pick and choose the activities based on the needs and developmental levels of your students. Answers for the activity pages are reproducible, so you may choose to give your students the activity pages as well as the answer page to let them progress on their own. The answers are on page 120.

## Extensions

- Ask students to write a letter to someone they admire. This can be a famous person, a friend, or a family member. They may write to a person living or dead, or even to a fictional character. Encourage students to write how they admire this person and what he or she means to them.

- Students can choose two characters from books, movies, or television and create a letter that one character might write to the other. The letter can be about the story, movie, or television show or about what happened that day.

- Invite each student to choose one person from fiction or nonfiction. Then each student can write a letter as if he or she were the character. The letter writer may not state his or her character's identity, but the writer should provide some clues so students can figure out who the character is. The other students must guess what character wrote the letter. The student who guesses correctly can then have his or her character's letter read aloud.

Name _____

# Student Study Pages

## Writing Letters

### Letter to a Friend

The **heading** may give the writer's address as well as the date. The **greeting** states to whom the letter is being written. The **body** of the letter presents the writer's message, and the **closing** is a way to say goodbye. The **signature** tells the person receiving the letter who wrote it. In a friendly letter, usually only the first name is given.

Monday, June 3

Dear Marisa,

    It was so good to see you at the park the other day. It's been a long time. How have you been? Have you seen our friend Jerome lately? What's he up to?

    I'm having a few people over for dinner next week. Would you like to come? Please let me know. I would love to see you.

Fondly,
Sharene

### Business Letter

A business letter is more formal and is often written flush left—heading, inside address, greeting, body of letter, closing, and signature all at the left-hand margin.

    The **heading** includes the date and the writer's address. The **inside address** includes the title of the person to whom the letter is being sent and his or her address. The **greeting** is more formal than in a friendly letter and includes the name and title of the person receiving the letter. If the name or title is not known, he or she may be addressed as *Dear Sir or Madam* or *To Whom It May Concern*. The greeting is followed by a colon (:). The **body** of a business letter contains the message, written more formally than a friendly letter. The **closing** is more formal as well. The most common closings are *Sincerely yours, Sincerely, Yours truly,* or *Cordially*. The **signature** usually includes the writer's name handwritten beneath the closing and then printed or typed out below that.

reproducible

*102*

© Good Apple GA13081

## Student Study Pages *continued*

4540 Sacramento Blvd.
Napa, CA 94558
June 3, 2001

Sirs Import and Export, Inc.
798 Hogan Street
Newark, NJ 12345

To Whom It May Concern:

I have not received the three cartons of heirloom seeds I ordered from your company three weeks ago. I would appreciate it if this problem could be taken care of as soon as possible.

Sincerely yours,

Carol Stradley

Carol Stradley

Name _____

# Letter-Writing Fun 1

**Directions:** Imagine that you are a product that is advertised on television. Write a business letter to the advertising agency, complaining about the commercial. Remember that you are writing the letter from the viewpoint of the product being advertised.

_____

_____

_____

_____

_____

_____

_____

_____

_____

_____

_____

_____

_____

_____

_____

_____

_____

_____

_____

_____

Name_____

# Letter-Writing Fun 2

**Directions:** Imagine that you are an object ordinarily found in a school classroom. Write a friendly letter to a student in which you complain about your living conditions. Remember that you are writing the letter from the viewpoint of the object.

_____

_____

_____

_____

_____

_____

_____

_____

_____

_____

_____

_____

_____

_____

_____

_____

_____

_____

_____

_____

_____

_____

Name _____

# Letter-Writing Fun 3

**Directions:** Imagine that you are a household appliance that has a malfunctioning part. Write a business letter to the company in which you complain about your malfunctioning part. Remember that you are writing the letter from the viewpoint of the appliance.

_____

_____

_____

_____

_____

_____

_____

_____

_____

_____

_____

_____

_____

_____

_____

_____

_____

_____

_____

Name_____

# Letter-Writing Fun 4

**Directions:** Choose a storybook character that you think your friend best resembles. Write a letter to your friend telling why you think he or she resembles this storybook character. Exchange letters with your friend.

_____
_____
_____
_____
_____
_____
_____
_____
_____
_____
_____
_____
_____
_____
_____
_____
_____
_____
_____
_____
_____

Name_____

# Letter-Writing Fun 5

**Directions:** Choose a person you know to whom you would like to write a letter and from whom you would like to receive a letter in return. Write a letter to him or her and enclose a stamped self-addressed envelope with your letter. Be sure to ask them to write back!

People to write to:

A famous person

Members of government about a particular issue

Someone with information on a topic in which you are interested

A friend or relative

A pen pal

_____

_____

_____

_____

_____

_____

_____

_____

_____

_____

_____

_____

_____

_____

Student's Name _____

# Assessment Tool Progress Report

**Progress**

_____
_____
_____
_____

**Improvement**

_____
_____
_____
_____

**Comments**

_____
_____
_____
_____

# Student Evaluation Progress Report

Student's name _____

| Punctuation and Sentences | Date | Teacher comments and/or suggestions |
|---|---|---|
| 1. Punctuation Riddles 1 | | |
| 2. Punctuation Riddles 2 | | |
| 3. Punctuation Fun 1 | | |
| 4. Punctuation Fun 2 | | |
| 5. Ridiculous Sentences 1 | | |
| 6. Ridiculous Sentences 2 | | |
| 7. Ridiculous Sentences 3 | | |
| 8. Ridiculous Sentences 4 | | |
| 9. Ridiculous Sentences 5 | | |
| 10. Scrambled Sentences 1 | | |
| 11. Scrambled Sentences 2 | | |
| 12. Brainstorming Sentences 1 | | |
| 13. Brainstorming Sentences 2 | | |
| 14. Generating Sentences Game 1 | | |
| 15. Generating Sentences Game 2 | | |
| 16. Generating Sentences Game 3 | | |
| 17. Generating Nonsense Alphabet Sentences Game | | |

| Punctuation and Sentences | Date | Teacher comments and/or suggestions |
|---|---|---|
| 18. Writing Tongue Twisters to Tangle Tongues 1 | | |
| 19. Writing Tongue Twisters to Tangle Tongues 2 | | |

| Ryhme and Poetry | Date | Teacher comments and/or suggestions |
|---|---|---|
| 20. Writing Nonsense Rhymes 1 | | |
| 21. Writing Nonsense Rhymes 2 | | |
| 22. Writing Nonsense Poems 1 | | |
| 23. Writing Nonsense Poems 2 | | |
| 24. Writing Limericks 1 | | |
| 25. Writing Limericks 2 | | |
| 26. Writing Limericks 3 | | |
| 27. Writing Limericks 4 | | |
| 28. Writing Limericks 5 | | |
| 29. Fun with Concrete Poetry | | |
| 30. Newspaper Poetry Writing Fun | | |
| 31. Cinquain Fun | | |
| 32. Haiku Fun | | |

## Student Evaluation Progress Report *continued*

| Challenges in Writing | Date | Teacher comments and/or suggestions |
|---|---|---|
| 33. Figure of Speech Riddles 1 | | |
| 34. Figure of Speech Riddles 2 | | |
| 35. Simile Fun 1 | | |
| 36. Simile Fun 2 | | |
| 37. Metaphor Fun 1 | | |
| 38. Metaphor Fun 2 | | |
| 39. Personification Fun 1 | | |
| 40. Personification Fun 2 | | |
| 41. Hyperbole Fun | | |
| 42. Oxymoron Fun 1 | | |
| 43. Oxymoron Fun 2 | | |
| 44. Compound Words Fun 1 | | |
| 45. Compound Words Fun 2 | | |
| 46. Descriptive Word Fun | | |
| 47. Descriptive Word Sentence Fun | | |
| 48. Word Endings Fun | | |
| 49. Homonym (Homophone) Sentence Fun 1 | | |

## Student Evaluation Progress Report *continued*

| Challenges in Writing | Date | Teacher comments and/or suggestions |
|---|---|---|
| 50. Homonym (Homophone) Sentence Fun 2 | | |
| 51. Homonym (Homophone) Sentence Fun 3 | | |

| Jokes, Tall Tales, and Stories | Date | Teacher comments and/or suggestions |
|---|---|---|
| 52. Writing Jokes 1 | | |
| 53. Writing Jokes 2 | | |
| 54. Writing Jokes 3 | | |
| 55. Writing Jokes 4 | | |
| 56. Fun with Tall Tales | | |
| 57. Fascinating Questions 1 | | |
| 58. Fascinating Questions 2 | | |
| 59. If I . . . | | |
| 60. Scrambled Animal Fun 1 | | |
| 61. Scrambled Animal Fun 2 | | |
| 62. Television-Writing Fun 1 | | |
| 63. Television-Writing Fun 2 | | |
| 64. Television-Writing Fun 3 | | |

| Jokes, Tall Tales, and Stories | Date | Teacher comments and/or suggestions |
|---|---|---|
| 65. Television-Writing Fun 4 | | |
| 66. Ridiculous Topics | | |
| 67. Short Story Ideas | | |
| 68. Nonsense Titles | | |
| 69. Ending a Story 1 | | |
| 70. Ending a Story 2 | | |
| 71. Completing a Story with Dialogue | | |

| WRITING LETTERS | Date | Teacher comments and/or suggestions |
|---|---|---|
| 72. Letter-Writing Fun 1 | | |
| 73. Letter-Writing Fun 2 | | |
| 74. Letter-Writing Fun 3 | | |
| 75. Letter-Writing Fun 4 | | |
| 76. Letter-Writing Fun 5 | | |

# Answers

## Punctuation and Sentences

### Student Review for Punctuation and Sentences (pages 9 and 10)

**Punctuation**

1. Though I didn't care, I still wanted to go.
2. Hey! Watch where you're going!
3. Jose said, "I'm not doing that, Mom."
4. Is that yours, Jane's, or mine?
5. "I'm not going to tell you," said Jack, "even if you beg."
6. "Who are you talking to?" asked Sarah as she turned to look behind her.

**Combining Sentences**

1. I would like to go to college, but my grades are not as good as I would like.
2. I know I can work harder at my studies and get better grades.

**Shortening Sentences**

1. Ty, Sasha, and Jenny like to cook.
2. Salvatore, Jake, and Tiffany are in a book club together.

**Independent and Dependent Word Groups**

1. Val loves the rain <u>because it helps her plants grow.</u>
2. Anahid's Dad drove Caitlin to her house <u>when she needed a ride.</u>

**Combining Independent and Dependent Word Groups**

1. We didn't drink the tea, although we were thirsty.
2. They can get better seats if they get to the concert early.

**Adjectives and Adverbs**

1. Gregory is funny, but Katie is the funniest.
2. The exciting play was performed wonderfully by the cast.

### Punctuation Riddles 1 (page 14)

1. b (Unnecessary information is set off by commas. In answer b, *Molly* is set off by commas because it is unnecessary information—there is only one sister.)
2. b
3. b
4. b
5. b

### Punctuation Riddles 2 (page 15)

1. a
2. b
3. a
4. b
5. a

### Punctuation Fun 1 (page 16)

1. Mother, the plumber, fixed the leak.
2. Private? No. Entry at any time.
3. The teacher called the students names as they entered the bus.
4. Stop! People on the highway.
5. Pardon; impossible to be sent back to jail.

### Punctuation Fun 2 (page 17)

1. Jack, the judge, said that we could go.
2. I'm not, stupid.
3. Mr. Stein, my teacher gives too many exams.
4. My sister Cara will be visiting Florida. (Since there are many sisters, no comma is used to set off *Cara*. No commas are used because *Cara* limits or restricts the noun *sister*. *Cara* tells you which sister will be visiting Florida. If there is only one sister, commas are used to set off *Cara*, because *Cara* is additional information.)
5. After the ball game we can eat Susan.

### Ridiculous Sentences 1 (page 18)

Answers may vary. Nonrestrictive participial phrases may precede subjects, and commas are omitted from restrictive phrases.

1. The man, smoking a pipe, ran after the dog.
2. The child, chewing gum, is bouncing the ball.
3. The girl, crying uncontrollably, looked for her sweater.
4. The man, wrapped in a towel, answered the phone.
5. Jack, smiling broadly, bought a new car.

### Ridiculous Sentences 2 (page 19)

Answers may vary.

1. The little girl, eating candy, walked into the store.
2. The speaker, twitching nervously, gave his lecture.
3. The father, carrying the baby, purchased a great quantity of groceries.
4. John, eating popcorn, watched the movie.

### Ridiculous Sentences 3 (page 20)

Answers may vary.

1. My hand, shivering from the cold, felt warm in my pocket.
2. Roberto, with itchy eyes, planted the tree.
3. Mr. Kinney, talking continuously, boarded the bus.
4. The baby, crying hysterically, banged the carriage.
5. The student, chewing gum, wrote on the chalkboard.

### Ridiculous Sentences 4 (page 21)

Answers may vary.

1. The child, burning with fever, was put in the ambulance.
2. Sherry, eating an ice-cream cone, walked down the street.
3. Mr. Dupont, wearing a bathing suit, mowed his lawn.
4. The girl, laughing aloud, picked up the phone.
5. Mrs. McGregor, breathing heavily, climbed the stairs.

### Ridiculous Sentences 5 (page 22)

Answers may vary.

1. Emma, holding her books, jumped over the rope.
2. Mr. Hoskins, perspiring from the heat, took a drink from the water fountain.
3. The little girl, singing a song, drew with chalk on the sidewalk.
4. The mail carrier, coughing excessively, put the mail in the box.
5. Sarah, chewing gum, worked on the computer.

### Scrambled Sentences 1 (page 23)

1. April showers bring May flowers.
2. Rats desert a sinking ship.
3. All that glitters is not gold.
4. Look before you leap.
5. Barking dogs seldom bite.
6. People are known by the company they keep.
7. One person's meat is another person's poison.
8. Don't let the grass grow under your feet.
9. Nothing succeeds like success.

### Scrambled Sentences 2 (page 24)

1. Beauty is only skin deep.
2. A stitch in time saves nine.
3. The early bird catches the worm.
4. Too many cooks spoil the broth.
5. An ape in king's clothing is still an ape.
6. Big trees from little acorns grow.
7. Don't judge a book by its cover.
8. It's an ill wind that blows no one any good.
9. Don't put all your eggs in one basket.

### Brainstorming Sentences 1 (page 25)

Sentences will vary.

### Brainstorming Sentences 2 (page 26)

Sentences will vary.

### Generating Sentences Game 1 (page 27)

Sentences will vary.

### Generating Sentences Game 2 (page 28)

Sentences will vary.

### Generating Sentences Game 3 (page 29)

Sentences will vary.

**Generating Nonsense Alphabet Sentences Game (page 30)**

Sentences will vary.

**Writing Tongue Twisters to Tangle Tongues 1 (page 31)**

Tongue twisters will vary.

**Writing Tongue Twisters to Tangle Tongues 2 (page 32)**

Tongue twisters will vary.

# Rhyme and Poetry

## Writing Nonsense Rhymes 1 (page 38)

Rhymes may vary. Here are some sample rhymes.

1. It bumped its head.
2. Then it jumped on the mat.
3. He pulled off my cap.
4. It scurried into its pen.
5. He scratched it with a pin.

## Writing Nonsense Rhymes 2 (page 39)

Rhymes may vary. Here are some sample rhymes.

1. "I need my sleep."
2. Then it rang the bell.
3. It turned to lead.
4. Then it flew into my father's den.
5. It wasn't very strong.

## Writing Nonsense Poems 1 (page 40)

(Sample last two lines)

I fear I'd better drop the song
Of butterfly and flowersong.

Nonsense poems will vary.

## Writing Nonsense Poems 2 (page 41)

(Sample last two lines)

 I guess I'd better skip the whir
Of anterpark and parkmeter.

Nonsense poems will vary.

## Writing Limericks 1 (page 42)

Lines will vary.

## Writing Limericks 2 (page 43)

(Limericks by Edward Lear)

(Sample last two lines)

1. He replied, "Yes, it does!
2. It's a regular brute of a bee!"

## Writing Limericks 3 (page 44)

(Limericks by Edward Lear)

(Sample last two lines)

1. The physician said this
2. "To a roast leg of mutton you may go."

## Writing Limericks 4 (page 45)

(Limericks by Edward Lear)

(Sample last two lines)

1. Four Larks and a Wren,
2. Have all built their nests in my beard!"
1. He said, "Certainly not,
2. He's my Mopsikon Flopsikon bear."

## Writing Limericks 5 (page 46)

Limericks will vary.

**Fun with Concrete Poetry (page 47)**

Concrete poems will vary..

**Newspaper Poetry Writing Fun (page 48)**

Newspaper poems will vary.

**Cinquain Fun (page 49)**

Cinquain poems will vary.

**Haiku Fun (page 50)**

Haiku poems will vary.

# Challenges in Writing

## Figure of Speech Riddles 1 (page 56)

1. Head; head of the class
2. Tree; family tree
3. Neck; bottleneck
4. Straw; last straw
5. Lap or leg; last lap *or* leg of the journey
6. Ladder; ladder of success

## Figure of Speech Riddles 2 (page 57)

1. Hands; hands of the clock
2. Apple of his eye *or* Adam's apple
3. Bed of roses
4. Millstone around my neck
5. Wild-goose chase
6. Shoulder; give the cold shoulder

## Simile Fun 1 (page 58)

1. c  2. g  3. j  4. b  5. d  6. h  7. e
8. f  9. a  10. i

## Simile Fun 2 (page 59)

Answers will vary.

## Metaphor Fun 1 (page 60)

1. g  2. d  3. f  4. c  5. a  6. e  7. b
8. j  9. h  10. i

## Metaphor Fun 2 (page 61)

1. d  2. c  3. h  4. j  5. b  6. a  7. f
8. i  9. g  10. e

## Personification Fun 1 (page 62)

1. e  2. b  3. g  4. j  5. c  6. d  7. a
8. f  9. i  10. h

## Personification Fun 2 (page 63)

Answers will vary.

## Hyperbole Fun (page 64)

Answers will vary.

## Oxymoron Fun 1 (page 65)

Oxymorons may vary. Here are some sample answers.

1. at the dawn of night
2. the living dead
3. a poor little rich girl
4. sweet sorrow
5. victory was defeating

## Oxymoron Fun 2 (page 66)

Answers will vary.

## Compound Words Fun 1 (page 67)

1. Eyeglasses
2. Headline
3. Necklace
4. Toothpick
5. Football

Sentences will vary.

## Compound Words Fun 2 (page 68)

1. Handout
2. Chestnut
3. Heartburn
4. Backyard
5. Necktie

Sentences will vary.

## Descriptive Word Fun (page 69)

Answers will vary.

## Descriptive Word Sentence Fun (page 70)

Answers will vary.

## Word Endings Fun (page 71)

Sentences will vary.

1. Actor
2. Player
3. Politely
4. Tricky
5. Nicely
6. Charmingly
7. Princely
8. Freedom
9. Fairly

## Homonym (Homophone) Sentence Fun 1 (page 72)

1. My eye hurt on the plane *or* plain.
2. I ate a whole steak.
3. Did you see the bear run into the woods?
4. I know that the way to Route 8 is not this way.
5. I wrote to my aunt to tell her son to write to me.

*118*

### Homonym (Homophone) Sentence Fun 2 (page 73)

1. I know that the ceiling has a leak.
2. My friend is a vain, lean person who likes to lay in the sun at the beach.
3. I ate currants, pears, and carrots.
4. The principal missed our class.
5. No one allowed the coarse person to enter our meeting.

### Homonym (Homophone) Sentence Fun 3 (page 74)

1. I am the sole person in the choral scene that does not sing.
2. I know two people who lie a lot.
3. No one will buy the coral canvas tent because it has an odd scent.
4. The principal in our main building does not know our needs.
5. Eight workers on loan from one other school were sent to fix our building.

# Jokes, Tall Tales, and Stories

### Writing Jokes 1 (page 79)

Answers will vary. Here are some sample answers.

1. "No, I still have only two," replied the nephew.
2. Salesperson: "No, I can only count on my fingers."

### Writing Jokes 2 (page 80)

Answers will vary. Here are some sample answers.

1. "I believe that, because it's in my food, too."
2. "You're right, but I didn't want to fail you."

### Writing Jokes 3 (page 81)

Answers will vary. Here are some Sample answers.

1. "No, because they haven't finished drinking this water yet."
2. "Gee, I didn't know silkworms could sew."

### Writing Jokes 4 (page 82)

Answers will vary. Here are some sample answers.

1. "I didn't know that you could make candy out of money." *or* "Oh, I hope they give out samples!"
2. "Then why do we ever have an energy crisis?" *or* "What happened before the law was passed?"

### Fun with Tall Tales (page 83)

Tall tales will vary.

### Fascinating Questions 1 (page 84)

Tall tales will vary.

### Fascinating Questions 2 (page 85)

Tall tales will vary.

### If I . . . (page 86)

Stories will vary.

### Scrambled Animal Fun 1 (page 87)

Answers will vary.

### Scrambled Animal Fun 2 (page 88)

Answers will vary.

### Television-Writing Fun 1 (page 89)

Answers will vary.

### Television-Writing Fun 2 (page 90)

Answers will vary.

### Television-Writing Fun 3 (page 91)

Answers will vary.

### Television-Writing Fun 4 (page 92)

Answers will vary.

### Ridiculous Topics (page 93)

Answers will vary.

### Short Story Ideas (page 94)

Stories will vary.

**Nonsense Titles (page 95)**

Stories will vary.

**Ending a Story 1 (page 96)**

Endings will vary.

**Ending a Story 2 (page 97)**

Endings will vary.

**Completing a Story with Dialogue (page 98)**

Endings will vary.

## Writing Letters

**Letter-Writing Fun 1 (page 104)**

Letters will vary.

**Letter-Writing Fun 2 (page 105)**

Letters will vary.

**Letter-Writing Fun 3 (page 106)**

Letters will vary.

**Letter-Writing Fun 4 (page 107)**

Letters will vary.

**Letter-Writing Fun 5 (page 108)**

Letters will vary.